100 FABULOUS MANDALAS FOR 12 YEARS OLD CHILDREN

creative mind

Jesus Ramirez

ISBN: 9798742338680

THANKS

To all the people who bought the book, and I hope you enjoy it.

ABOUT THE AUTHOR

My name is Jesus Ramirez, born in Caracoli, Antioquia on October 28, 1994, he attends all high school studies in my hometown, I have 2 male brothers, I lived with my mother Nelcy Gómez, my stepfather Jose Calderón and my brother Jhon Jairo Ramirez, my another brother Jose Ramirez recides in another city. At the age of 19 I migrated to the capital of the country Bogota Colombia where I am currently, with the passage of time I worked in different areas until one day I decided to become an Author since reading and writing have always caught my attention.